Antonio Montes Orozco

The Work Stress Cycle

A business fable about "coaching", "agilism" and the five steps that lead to burn out at work.

Table of Contents

Antonio Montes Orozco

Introduction

In the world of software, endless days are the routine. This causes workers to leave very late and return home without time for anything other than dinner and bedtime.

Imagine a life in a loop, in which one day dangerously resembles the next one, and the next one, and the next one... a life with hardly any time for anything other than work: no family, no friends, no recreational activity, which is so necessary to recharge batteries in this stressful world. That is the life that many workers have, and that many others have experienced at some point in their professional career.

Through this fable I pose the story of Robert, our protagonist, who is burned out for living in a continuously high-stress environment. Robert will discover what has led him to this situation and draw his own conclusions. You will discover the world of coaching, the world of "Agilism", and you will learn about the five steps that lead to entering the "Work Stress Cycle".

Burning out workers is counterproductive for the worker and for the company itself, so it is good to be aware of the price involved in overtime. Loading the members of a team with impossible tasks is the result of fear, so we will discover that we must eliminate fear from the equation.

Antonio Montes Orozco

Dedicated to:

Rosa, my indefatigable companion and the fruit of our love:

Elena and Laura

Antonio Montes Orozco

Chapter 1: An Unsustainable Situation

Robert

Our story begins with Robert, a young man of thirty-four years old, of medium height, curly and brown hair, and overweight. He is a programmer analyst who has been working in the software world for ten years. He studied Software Engineering, and when he graduated at twenty-four years old he quickly found a job. Since then, he knew the preoccupations of the software world: projects that were twisted, and extra hours that were worked, without receiving remuneration in return, and leaving him in a pitiful state of exhaustion. In addition, the fatigue was so extreme that the coffees were no longer effective, and he made many mistakes during the workday. These mistakes had to be remedied, so that meant more work and more overtime. Until the project was delivered to the client, Robert was in a panic to go through the same situation over and over again.

In addition, the way of working seemed absurd: in each project, a project manager was appointed who directed all the work. Before knowing anything about the product to be designed, they tried to document everything thoroughly, even though it was impossible to have so much detail, and the client did not even know what they wanted. After the initial titanic effort to document the entire product, everything was subdivided into tasks. Some were absurd tasks that would never be done, as they were based on an incorrect vision of the product. Reality always imposes changes, and it is very difficult to adapt these changes to the original plan.

This obsession to adapt to the initial plan leads to the loss of market opportunities, and to design products that were not what the client really wanted. It was very frustrating that, after so much effort invested, the client was dissatisfied with the product shown.

Robert still remembered that client who sold second-hand cars: He asked for an application to show the cars he had in store. A competitor invested in developing a similar application, which clients could easily access, showing their driver's license to the camera. Robert's client was left without his own simple access, because his was preset and the contract was signed; thus, after a year, he was given an application inferior to that one that the competitor had, to everyone's disappointment.

Robert, over the years, had met bosses who took into account the opinion of the programmers and trusted their criteria, but he had also met others who distrusted the programmers and treated them as lazy, regardless of their criteria and managing all tasks dictatorially. Any deviation from the plan set was attributed to the poor performance of the programmers, so they were punished with working overtime. These work peaks led to extreme fatigue of the entire team, and they made more mistakes, so the ball was getting bigger and bigger, to everyone's frustration.

During those years, not everything was bad, because he met Victoria, his wife, and married her. Victoria was cheerful, and a faithful and committed companion. Robert went out of his way for her, but, after longer work days, he came home so late that he was frustrated, feeling completely empty and exhausted.

There were also bad economic cycles that impoverished the country; the companies began to have losses and sometimes Robert was laid off, so he had to look for a job, to the despair of the young couple.

With the last crisis Robert was laid off again and ended up in the company where he was currently working. The work methodology was the same as always, and the project manager, Gerard, was the worst of all he'd had so far. He was just as dictatorial as the rest, but he listened less to his team and imposed impossible deadlines, so that each of his projects ended with anger and overtime, to the frustration of the team of programmers. The company where Victoria worked also went into crisis, and she lost her job, so she was now unemployed and looking for job offers every day.

Robert went back into a dynamic of overtime and extreme exhaustion. His health suffered and eventually ended up with a cold that did not get better, and instead worsened day by day. He was so exhausted that he could no longer have any down time with Victoria, as he fell asleep, literally speaking. Victoria felt that Robert was no longer listening to her. They couldn't even watch any of their favorite television series, which they enjoyed sharing when things were going well. After a while, her day was reduced to looking for a job in the morning and seeing her husband's shadow in the afternoon, with whom she could not speak. The love she felt for Robert faded away and she became disenchanted with their relationship, which Robert began to noticed with alarm.

Although the situation was very tense and Robert's project was in danger of ending badly, he decided to go to the doctor and take care of himself, because he began to be afraid that his marriage would be broken, and that his cold would become complicated and end up in an ear infection. In addition, he had gained weight dangerously in recent months; so he decided to ask Gerard for time off to visit the doctor.

Visit to the doctor

Robert had arrived at the doctor's half an hour earlier, hoping to be seen at the time of his appointment, nine thirty in the morning. But to Robert's despair, the doctor was late, as always. With a delay of one hour, the doctor finally treated him. Robert opened the door doubtfully and found, seated behind a cherrywood desk, a young man in a white coat. He had brown amber hair, wearing it a bit long and rumpled, and showed a three-day beard that gave him the appearance of a meditative philosopher.

"Good morning, I'm the Doctor Serene. Sit down, please."

"Good morning, Doctor."

"How can I help you? Tell me what's bothering you."

"The thing is that I'm exhausted. I've been in the middle of a work crisis for several weeks, and I can't stand it anymore. I have a never ending cold; I've gained a lot of weight; and, even worse, I do nothing but argue with my wife."

"I see. I note that you've got many dark circles. How many hours do you sleep daily?"

"I turn off the bedside light at two o'clock in the morning, and get up at six o'clock, so I sleep about four hours."

"Of course, those are very few hours. Sleeping is necessary, and the lack of sleep has got more consequences than people think. For example, defenses go down and we get sick more easily: that would explain the cold you talk about. The other consequence is that the endocrine system is deregulated, and we tend to gain more weight: that would explain why you've gained weight. The last consequence is that it makes us forget the good things, so we remember only the negative things that happen to us during the day: that brings us to a depressive state. It doesn't explain why you're arguing with your wife, but perhaps all these things have contributed to a bad mood these days."

Antonio Montes Orozco

"Well, now that you mention it, I am more negative these days. In fact, everything seems to be bothersome," replied Robert enthusiastically, feeling understood for the first time.

"Look, I'm examining you right now, but you should tidy up your life." The doctor listened to Robert's chest and looked at his ears and throat." For now, don't worry, because you don't need antibiotics yet, but if you keep on sleeping poorly, you will surely complicate your cold and I will have to prescribe them to you."

"But I can't avoid my work load. I'm the only salary that enters my house. My wife doesn't work," replied Robert, overwhelmed.

"I see. I'm very sorry. I imagine that you'll be drinking coffee all day to stay awake."

Robert nods, as if the doctor had read his thoughts.

"And do you have the coffee with sugar?"

"Yeah, of course. Very few people can drink it black: it tastes very bitter."

"I wanted to get there. Every time you have sugar, it provokes a peak of glucose into the body. Glucose is energy, after all. Glucose is the energy consumed by the brain or muscles. If you don't play sports immediately after consuming it, you won't have time to spend so much glucose. But the body has a mechanism to remove glucose from the body and prevent you from suffering from hyperglycemia: it orders your pancreas to produce insulin."

"Excuse me, doctor," snapped Robert, "but I do not know what hyperglycemia is."

"Yeah, you are right. I'm using medical terms without explaining myself. Hyperglycemia is excess of glucose in your blood. In the long term it can cause death or blindness. Have you heard of diabetes?"

"Yes, but I don't know what it is."

"Well, diabetes is a disease of the pancreas. It cannot produce insulin, so the body cannot remove the glucose from the blood, so it accumulates with disastrous consequences. If you are constantly producing insulin, in the end it ends up damaging the pancreas and it stops working. Or your cells may end up being resistant to insulin, so it isn't as effective and stops removing the excess of glucose from the body. Therefore, it is not good to force the body. Everything must be done in moderation. Don't consume sugar all day, like in the coffee you drink, or you'll end up diabetic."

"Very well, doctor. But I didn't know anything about this."

"I know it. It isn't your fault. But that's why, nowadays, so many people are dying from stroke, heart attack, and diabetes. And it's a shame. It isn't to alarm you, but everything has consequences. If you wish, I can recommend you a book that I know that explains all this in a very simple way, so that you can learn it and understand it. This way it'll cost you less effort to sacrifice the sugar of the coffees you have." The doctor gave Robert a paper with the title of a book and its author written down. "And, have you thought about trying to change your job?"

"Well, I really haven't had time to think about it, to tell you the truth."

"Look, I'm just a doctor and I can't help you anymore. I've already told you the consequences of not sleeping and having too much sugar. Maybe you should visit a coach. They have become very fashionable, and people end up very happy with them."

"Aren't they the ones who train tennis players or soccer teams? Do you want me to play sports? Am I that out of shape?"

"Ha, ha, ha, ha, ha, ha, ha!" Laughed the doctor sincerely. "No, the coach is a person who listens to you carefully, and then asks you questions, so that you can clarify ideas. But I think they are expensive. They can cost 120 dollars an hour."

"My God! I think it's very expensive, doctor!" Robert is alarmed because, with his wife being unemployed, money is an issue.

"Yeah, but if you don't clean up your life, you'll increasingly destroy yourself. And the next time I see you, it'll be to send you an antibiotic prescription. In addition, obesity brings nothing but problems. Have you heard of strokes and heart attacks?"

"Yeah, sure. But I don't know what relationship they have between them."

"Well, look, in both cases, a deposit of fat in our veins or arteries moves and travels through the body until it stops, clogging an artery, for example. The artery, being clogged, stops sending food and oxygen to the surrounding cells, so they die. If that artery is in the brain, we suffer a stroke. If that artery is in the heart, we suffer a heart attack. You are somewhat overweight, and that means you must have high levels of cholesterol. That is, a fat deposit is being created somewhere in your body, which can give you problems in the future. Look, to be sure, I'm going to order you a blood test. Come as soon as you have the results, and we'll see how you are doing. Here you are, the referral note."

"Thanks a lot, doctor!"

"You're welcome. See you, and think about the coach."

Robert left the office thoughtful. "If I have a stroke or heart attack because of work stress, what would happen to Vicky?" He could also suffer a hyperglycemia or diabetes. He wasn't a doctor and didn't understand even half of the things the doctor had said, but he did know cases of diabetes, and didn't want to suffer from it, if he could avoid it. He was also scared of the issue of a stroke. Vicky was too young and didn't deserve a husband with a stroke. In addition, he had heard cases of many people ending up invalid and unable to work, or had to relearn to walk, or to write, or even to speak. He had also heard the case of people suffering from a heart attack: they were so bad that they always ended up dying because of the heart. No. Definitely, Robert did not want that for his wife. But when could he go to see the coach? And when would he go to do the blood tests? He hated having to ask Gerard for time off. He was in crunch time at work and didn't have time. He came home every day at ten o'clock. He should have studied something else, but the truth is that he couldn't think of anything different from Computer Engineering. Since he was a teenager, he had always been interested in computers and programming.

He would search in the Internet for a coach who practiced in his area and try. He had nothing to lose, and, if the doctor said so, it would be for something. It was a somewhat unusual recipe. Sending him a book to read was also awkward, but his life was currently chaos, and he had to put an end to that situation. He was scared of a stroke, a heart attack, and diabetes. Suddenly, health and being with Victoria were the really important matters. The project he was currently working on had lost importance, and he even saw it as something that could destroy his life.

How had it all started? When did he start arguing with Vicky? He only knew that he'd felt misunderstood by her for a few months. He was exhausted, and she only complained about how alone she was, and that the housework fell on her. Even when he had made an effort to watch a movie on TV with her, he had also made her angry, because, in the end, Robert had fallen asleep. But it wasn't his fault: he was broken and couldn't stand it anymore. In addition, the work was complicated, and everyone on the team made many mistakes. The application they were programming was full of flaws and did nothing but fail. It was very frustrating not being able to move forward, and having to constantly resolve the bugs that appeared.

That day he was so sad that he decided to call his best friend, Arthur, or Arty, as he used to call him. Arthur was very big, bordering on obesity, and he was always happy; he was about Robert's age and had studied Psychology, so he often laughed at Robert and his typical masculine behaviors. He always told him that he had very little "emotional intelligence", to which Robert always responded by getting angry: he had a degree in Engineering and was very intelligent, so he also had "emotional intelligence". One day, Arthur made him open his eyes and realize his mistake.

"Let's see, Rob, put yourself in your wife's place: all day at home, looking for a job and alone, wanting to talk to someone. And, at night, a tired husband arrives, who doesn't speak or communicate, and who only thinks about watching a movie, which prevents communication. Do you still think that you're showing 'emotional intelligence'?" snapped Arthur.

"THEY ARE NOT MOVIES; THEY ARE TV SERIES!" answered Robert sulkily. "In addition, they're very relaxing, and funny!" Robert continued, somewhat calmer.

"Let's see, Rob, they're relaxing for you, because you're a hunter and, when you're tired, what relaxes you is hunting. But Vicky is a gatherer, and what relaxes her is gathering. Therefore, talk to her, and you will see how she receives you with open arms, and you will feel so happy that you will realize that it is worth a thousand times more than watching any fashion series. In addition, watching television totally breaks communication."

"But Arty, have you gone crazy? What is it that thing that I'm a hunter and Vicky a gatherer?" asks Robert without understanding anything at all.

"Well, it is a very famous idea that is beginning to gain ground in common society. Evolutionarily speaking, men are hunters, because they went out to hunt in prehistory, while women are gatherers, because they went out to collect through the forest, to see what they found. That can give you an idea of why men relax by concentrating on one thing, such as watching TV, for example, which would be equivalent to hunting, and why women relax gathering, concentrating on several things at once, talking and sharing experiences."

"However, I think that our romance is fading and that Vicky doesn't love me anymore. I'm not sure I love her either. Love is gone."

Antonio Montes Orozco

"YOU SHUT UP WITH THAT FALSE IDEA THAT LOVE CAN GO AND COME!" Arthur jumped like a spring. "False and very harmful ideas that crush us are getting into society. Well, look, I'm going to tell you a secret: love doesn't come or go, but it is a state of self-induced autosuggestion, just like religious faith."

"How is that, Arty? Now I don't understand anything."

"Well, for you to understand, we decide on what to have faith and whom to love: that would go into self-induction. We program ourselves to have faith and to love someone: that would enter into autosuggestion. You met Victoria and you liked her a lot, both because you liked her physically and because of how happy she made you. I still remember the silly face you wore every time you saw her. At that moment you decided to love her and asked her out on a date. Therefore, love her and let everything return to its path. Talk to her, meet her, take care about how she feels, discover what she likes and dislikes, wish to share time with her with all your strength. That's what you did when she caught your attention years ago, and you decided to love her. Therefore, love does not come and go, but we decide. So, decide to love her and do not throw these years in the trash. Who will know you better than her? Who will want to be with you when you are an old man? Who else would you form a family with? I don't understand how such a harmful and stupid idea has penetrated society so much. Did you know that two-thirds of couples end up breaking up because of this harmful idea?"

Antonio Montes Orozco

"I understand you. I'm looking forward to getting home to rediscover my Vicky."

"That's what I've always liked about you, Rob, that you pick out ideas straight away, and understand them instantly. You're going to reach very far."

"But I'm afraid that Vicky is one of the victims of that idea and she also believes that our love is gone."

"NOOOOOOO, ROB! ELIMINATE FEAR FROM THE EQUATION! You're the smartest guy I've ever met!" Arthur was upset, to Robert's surprise. "If there is a basis for your fears, you will get ahead of this and reinvent yourself, as you have always done! And, if there is no basis, why worry? Forget your fears and decide what you want to do, trust your intuition, and do it!"

"Well, Arty, don't get like that. I didn't mean for you to get so upset!"

"Come on, come here and give me a hug."

The two friends said goodbye with a big hug. Robert liked Arthur very much. He knew how to put sanity back in the crazy world around him, and always had the right words to help.

That night, when Robert arrived home, Victoria was waiting for him with a sad face, as was the custom lately.

Victoria

"Hi, honey, I'm home now," said Robert cheerfully.

"Hi Rob. What did the doctor tell you?" replied Victoria, eager to have some conversation.

"Well, he ordered me a blood test, and told me to sleep more, because it seems that part of what happens to me has to do with not sleeping enough hours. He told me that not sleeping causes your body to lower its defenses, so you get ill; that you gain weight, so you increase the risk of stroke or heart attack; and that you see everything negatively and get depressed. And then, apart from strokes and heart attacks, he scared me with diabetes. I mean, he painted everything very black. He's also recommended me a book where all these topics are discussed."

"Well, you'll have to listen to him, honey. I want to grow old with you, Rob. And what are you going to do?"

"So, honey, have you decided to love me? Have you self-induced to autosuggest loving me?" Robert couldn't restrain his enthusiasm to discover that Victoria still loved him.

"Ha, ha, ha, ha, ha!" laughed his wife. "What's happened to you at work? Why are you talking crazy?"

"I've really been talking to Arty, and it's been very good for me. He has opened my eyes, as he always does. I will ask Gerard for permission to go to do the analytics. I will end this topic. Oh, and Dr. Serene has given me interesting information about people who are coach, and who help you clarify ideas."

"What, those who train soccer teams?"

"No, ha, ha, ha, ha!" laughs Robert loudly. "Although I'm fat, I'm not going to play sports. Coaches listen to you, ask you questions, and help you clarify ideas."

"But what are they, counselors?"

"Well, that's funny; no, they aren't. The doctor made it sound as though they know nothing."

"I don't think you're going to be worse than you are now. Why don't you give such a coach a try?"

"Well, because they cost $120 an hour."

"It's horrible, Rob! I feel so bad for not bringing money home. I didn't know it was so expensive," exclaimed Victoria, feeling guilty.

"Do not worry, honey. We have money saved for something like this. As you say, I'm not going to be worse. I don't mind having 120 bucks less of savings. Tomorrow I'm calling a coach who works close to home, and I'll schedule an appointment. By the way, what do you think about sitting down to have dinner quietly, putting on relaxing music, and chatting comfortably on the sofa? I don't know how long I'll hold up awake, but at least we'll have talked a bit until I fall asleep.

Arty has made me see that, if you are alone all day, you need to talk."

"Well, thank Arty. It's just what I needed. You can't imagine how hard the day is on me without being able to talk to anyone, except those of human resources people who call me, taking an interest in me."

"Sure, I'll thank him: he is a good friend, although he easily gets irritated." The image of Arthur came to Robert's mind, thinking about when he was outraged by the harmful ideas that were introduced into society. "By the way, he's told me a phrase that has caught my attention. He's told me to 'eliminate fear from the equation.'"

"Of course, it is what I've always told you, that you're afraid and that blocks you. Fear is not good for making decisions."

"Vicky, I'm realizing that you're going to be my teacher in this matter of 'emotional intelligence', because I see that you've got a lot. And you're right, I anticipate a lot and I'm anxious about things that haven't happened yet."

"I don't know what has happened to you, but I love seeing you like this." Victoria hugged Robert, very happy to see her husband so communicative.

That evening, Robert fell asleep again, but they talked for several hours until this happened, which was like a breath of fresh air for Victoria. She helped her husband go to bed and, after that, she stayed up reading for a while, happy with the change in direction the situation was going. Blessed Arty: he had taken advantage of his Psychology Degree, and now he gave private consultation at home, helping people.

The next day, Robert decided to take it seriously and asked his boss for permission to get a blood test. Gerard was not a good boss and was bad at planning the project. He had all his team demotivated and burned out. There were several fights when something failed, and too many things failed.

Unfortunately, it was a normal situation for Robert, since he had lived this way since he entered the workforce. But the visit to the doctor had scared him. He loved Victoria too much to leave her as a widow so young. Nothing in the world could justify the dog life he led. In addition, the conversation with Arty had opened his mind to new topics to explore, such as "emotional intelligence" and "eliminating fear from the equation".

Gerard

Robert waited for his boss to be in a good mood to ask permission to go for the blood test. That same morning, Gerard had gotten into a meeting to report on the project to his superiors. The project was being delayed, so Gerard was shut up with a deluge of difficult-to-answer questions. The rotation that reigned in the team was so great that it had reached the ears of the managers, which called into question Gerard's skills as a team leader. After having his morning coffee, he adopted a less irascible attitude so, at that time, Robert took the opportunity to ask him for permission. He entered Gerard's office hesitantly.

"Good morning, Gerard. I need to arrive a little late tomorrow morning to do some blood tests."

The project manager pouted and tried to manipulate him into feeling guilty.

"You'll know, Rob, this is not the moment to waste time on blood tests. The project is not going well, and everyone's hands are needed to move it forward. What will your colleagues think if you take the morning off?"

At that moment, Robert thought what his wife would think if he became seriously ill. The visit to the doctor had clarified his priorities a lot: no project was above his health. Suddenly, the answer came to his mind.

"Gerard, look at it this way: wouldn't it be better for the project that I recover quickly and not get sick? So that I can be one hundred percent with the team guys, taking the project forward."

"Man, seen like this, I buy you the idea. Well, good luck with the analysis."

"Thanks a lot, Gerard. You will see how, in the end, this is for the best." Robert was very proud of how he had managed the situation: not only had he managed to avoid being manipulated by Gerard, but he had also managed to remain as a proactive employee committed to the project. "Remember that tomorrow I arrive a bit late, but then I will make up for it in the afternoon."

"Don't worry, Rob, it's cool."

The next day Robert went to have the blood tests done and, taking advantage of that, he made an appointment for Dr. Serene to see him, and give him the results. The week continued progressing, and Robert left the office late every day. But now Robert knew what was wrong. He understood all the problems that sleeping few hours was causing him. His life consisted of getting up half asleep, having a strong coffee in the breakfast, going to work, enduring Gerard's bad manners, discovering the mistakes made the previous day, trying to solve them and, meanwhile, trying to finish the functionality that was pending of the application of PC they were developing.

In between, since he was going to leave late, he took refuge in numerous and endless moments of coffee breaks, where he dedicated to gossiping with his companions the different ways that Gerard had verbal abused them that day. In between, rare was the day when a teammate didn't warn that he had weeks left on the team, because he was shortly waiting for an offer from a competitor company. The rotation of personnel did a lot of damage, because the coworkers who were leaving took with them the knowledge, and is was very expensive to train the new teammates that arrived. But if they didn't devote time to training the new team members, they couldn't help, so, in the end, it was assumed that the new teammates had to be trained, even if it felt like a waste of time.

Within a week, Robert returned to the strange doctor's office:

"Good afternoon, Robert. I see you with much better appearance. You no longer have the dark circles you came with the first day I saw you. Are you sleeping more?" asked Dr. Serene good-naturedly.

"Yes, doctor. Not only that, but I'm very proud, because, without arguing, I managed to avoid being manipulated by my boss, who wanted to prevent me from doing the blood test. Now I have to read the book you recommended me, and visit the coach. The truth is that I'm very grateful to you for making the priorities clear to me."

"It's true! I forgot! I'd never had a patient so applied!" exclaimed the doctor. "Well, the book will explain the glucose cycle, and the coach may be very helpful to you. I see you very well, really. And regarding the blood test, you have high cholesterol, so you have to lose weight. I propose that other tests be done within six months, when you have lost weight, and so for now we remain calm, because I'm sure your cholesterol will also have dropped. From what I've discovered lately, people don't know anything about proper nutrition, and taking care of themselves to keep weight off. Therefore, I will recommend you another book, since I see that you are an open patient, where it will be explained how you should lead a healthy diet."

To Robert's amazement, the doctor gave him two papers: one was the reminder to have the analysis done in six months, and another was the title and author of another book, but this time on nutrition. "Well, see you in six months, and I hope you do very well. You are intelligent, you realize about things and you are a very applied patient, so I know you will do very well. Have a good afternoon."

"Thanks a lot, doctor! You are great!"

Robert couldn't believe it. It was so difficult to find such an exceptional doctor, that it was hard for him to believe he was so lucky. From being depressed and hopeless, he now had come to see the light. He was looking forward to visiting the coach and reading the two books that Dr. Serene had recommended: one on strokes, heart attacks, and diabetes; and the other one about nutrition.

When he got home, he was eager to talk to Victoria and share what had happened to him.

"Honey, I'm home now!" Robert greeted Victoria.

"Hi, my love. I see you very lively. Tell me what the doctor told you," replied Victoria, very happy to talk to someone.

"Well, you won't believe it, but he's recommended me another book! This time about nutrition. He must be the weirdest doctor in the city."

"Isn't he that one with a crazy goatee, and that has the hair a bit long and ruffled? I think he's called Doctor Tranquil or something," asked Victoria. "I saw him at the clinic the last time I went, and I liked his appearance. I wondered what kind of doctor he'd be and how he'd treat patients."

"He's called Serene, honey," pointed out Robert. "Well, I think he connects very well with the patient, and that his treatments are very novel. In addition, they seem to be effective. I will tell you, because I have to call a coach, and I have to start reading one of the two books that he has recommended me: the one of diabetes and strokes that he recommended me the other day, or the one of nutrition that he has recommended me today."

In front of Robert, a world of hope opened, because, apart from the fact that things were going better at home, and he had learned that he had to rest, reading the books and visiting the coach promised an even greater improvement in the situation.

But he was overwhelmed by the idea of having to give explanations at work, so he'd look for a coach who had consultations on Saturdays. He also didn't want to travel far to have the sessions, so he would investigate around his area. Regardless, he had to make decisions, 'eliminating fear from the equation'.

Chapter 2: Robert Visits The Coach

The coaching session

After searching the Internet, Robert found a coach close to his area. The reviews didn't say bad things about him. In addition, it happened that this coach worked on Saturday mornings, so no one at work would find out that he was going to visit him. He wouldn't endure the interrogation his coworkers would submit him to, and he wouldn't have to put up with Gerard berating him for missing work. So Robert decided to go and see the coach on a Saturday morning and avoid giving explanations in the office.

He decided to telephone him, and, to his delight, discovered that Stephen, the coach, was extremely pleasant. So he made an appointment with him and wrote down the address.

The day of the appointment Robert got up at eight, showered, had a coffee with milk and a chocolate muffin with dark chocolate chips for breakfast, and drove to the coach's house, who had a home office in a neighborhood near Robert's. He parked right in front of the house, which was Victorian style, and painted in a beautiful olive-green. He got out of the car and walked towards the door, following the garden path. He rang the bell and, in a few seconds, a tall black man with gray hair and good preserved looking opened the door. He was thin and, although he had a dynamic appearance, his gray hair showed a man well into his forties.

"Hello, good morning. You must be Robert. My name is Stephen."

"Hello, good morning. Yes, indeed, I am Robert. I've come to have a coaching session with you." Robert shakes hands with the coach.

"I'm glad you'd taken this step. Come in, please." He led Robert to an office located on the ground floor. The 'coachee' sat in a chair, while the 'coach' sat in the comfortable armchair behind his desk. "However, I am a certified coach. How can I help you?"

"Well, I've been very tired during the last weeks, due to a heavy workload. Overtime has led me to be sick, to gain weight, and to be in a bad mood, so I argue a lot with my wife. That's why I went to see the doctor, and he recommended that I come to have a coaching session with you."

"Did Doctor Serene send you? He's in the clinic you told me on the phone. He is the one with long, ruffled hair."

"Yes, that's him!" replied Robert enthusiastically, remembering the special way Dr. Serene had of taking care of his patients.

"I thought so." Stephen grinned broadly, as if he also remembered the doctor's original statements. "And do you know what this stuff of coaching is about?"

"Well, the doctor told me something, but he didn't say much. He told me that you would ask me questions and little else."

"Okay, let's see: the answers are inside you. No one better than you to find the solutions, because you, even if you don't know it, have all the necessary data. The only thing that happens to us is that we are not taught to ask ourselves the right questions. I will listen to you carefully, I will try to understand you and, by asking you simple questions, I will help you find the answers to your problems yourself. I am not a counselor, or anything like that, so don't expect me to advise you. Well, not quite: if I see that there's some path that you haven't considered or that you don't know, I may encourage you to explore it, but nothing else. I don't intend to manipulate you or guide you, but you have to be the one who realizes about things: that way you will commit to the decision you make, because there is a principle that says the following: 'Without involvement, there is no commitment.' Its author is one of my teachers: Stephen Covey. His name is the same as mine, and the truth is that I admire his work very much."

"It seems interesting. Anyway, we start whenever you wish."

"Great. First we have to formalize the session. To do this, I'll ask you to sign this contract, for which I agree not to disclose anything you tell me. A coach is like a confessor, or like a lawyer, or even like Dr. Serene who treated you. We are bound to nondisclosure agreements." He showed Robert the standard contract. "Look at it calmly and, if you agree, I would need you to sign it, in order to formalize the session."

Antonio Montes Orozco

Robert read the contract carefully. He would never have imagined so much formalism. Although, if someone was going to know his most intimate thoughts, it made sense that he was protected by professional privacy. On second thought, it didn't seem so weird.

"Sounds good to me," he said at the end.

"Great. So, whenever you want, you talk to me."

"Okay. I have a bachelor's degree in Computer Engineering, and became a programmer when obtaining the degree. From the beginning I worked overtime in all the jobs I went through. I didn't know anything else, and it seemed normal to me. In between I met my wife, Victoria; we got married, and, during these last months, I'm coming home very late and I feel exhausted. I also started with a cold that didn't get better, so I got scared, and went to see Dr. Serene. He told me that fatigue was lowering my defenses, which explained why I was ill; that it was making me overweight, which explained the extra pounds I had taken in recent months; and it was making me remember only the negative things, so it was taking me to a state of negativity that made me see everything black."

"And what time do you arrive home?"

"Well, at ten o'clock at night."

"And what do you do when you get home?"

"I usually have dinner with Vicky. After that, we usually watch a series on TV, but I always fall asleep. She got angry, because I'm just nodding while trying to find out what's going on in the episode we're watching. Then I try to read a little in bed, turning off the light at two, getting up again at six in the morning. There are times that, in the morning, Vicky reproaches me that she's been talking to me at night, and that I haven't answered her, so I understand that the fatigue has beaten me, and that being sleepy has messed up my relationship with my wife. But now, after talking with my friend Arty, I talk to her for a while and go to bed with a book, falling asleep at two in the morning."

"I'm surprised about your friend Arty. Tell me more about him, please."

"Arty is a psychologist and my best friend. Sometimes he easily gets irritated, and gives me a good fight, but thanks to him I have learned that, in life, you have to 'eliminate fear from the equation.' He's also advised me to talk to Vicky, because she's unemployed, and she spends all day alone at home, looking for a job."

"Your friend Arty seems very interesting to me. However, I understand that you only sleep four hours every day."

"Yeah, and that's what, according to Dr. Serene, leads me to gain weight, be negative, and have a weak health, as I told you before."

"By the way, like all branches of knowledge have their gurus, in this field of coaching I also follow a guru, named John Whitmore. He is the father of the **GROW** method, which is an acronym that comes from the words **G**oal, that is, what you want; **R**eality, or where you are now; **O**ptions, that is, what you could do; and **W**ill, or what you'll do. Therefore, let's start by defining your primary objective: How would you like to be?"

"Well, I'd like not to be so tired and be able to share more quality time with Vicky."

"Great. Now, let's explore the real situation you are in."

"Well, I have to work overtime, and I can't avoid it right now, because of the way we work, and because of the project manager we have. But, once I get home, I am free to decide how to use my time."

"Great, Robert! You are doing very well!" Exclaimed Stephen enthusiastically. "You're being realistic and you're realizing what depends on you and what doesn't. Let's explore the options you have."

"Well, going to another company, where I am sure that the situation will be repeated, as it's an inherent evil in software companies. I could change to another company, although I don't know how to do something different than programming, since I'm a computer engineer. And the last option I see is to change the way I work in my company, and prevent people from doing overtime, so that they aren't so tired and don't make so many mistakes. Part of our delay in deliveries is due to the lack of quality of the code, so we spend a lot of time fixing the mistakes we've made. Most of these are due to fatigue."

"And now the million-dollar question comes," said Stephen with excitement, "what are you going to do to avoid being so tired?"

"Well, I can think of two actions. The first one would be to sleep more, and avoid taking, from my sleeping time, the time I have to relax. The second one would be to get home earlier, as this is what would allow me to have some down time with Vicky."

"I see. By the way, since you talk about spending time with your wife, taking into account that you get home late, what kind of down time do you plan to have?"

"Well, as Arty has recommended me, chatting with my wife, since she's unemployed, and spends all day alone at home."

"Very good for your friend, really. And what are you going to do then?"

"Well, to start with, sleeping more to begin to recover myself. As soon as there is no more overtime and I'm recovered, devoting more time to Vicky. Today I rule out watching TV, as that cuts off communication between us, and talking is what she needs. I want to learn to have 'emotional intelligence', as my friend Arty has recommended me. By sleeping more, I would be fresher the following day, and I wouldn't make so many mistakes at work, so I wouldn't have to waste my time having to fix them, and I wouldn't be so stressed."

"Great, that sounds good. It is very easy to explore with you. I see you have taken to the trick of coaching very quickly. By the way, 'emotional intelligence' is something that is acquired inside the family. If you haven't learned it so far, the good news is that it can be learned. For this I recommend the book *Emotional Intelligence* by Daniel Goleman. It would also be great if you had someone close to you with emotional intelligence, so that you could learn by imitation."

"Vicky will be my teacher because in emotional intelligence she knows much more than I do!" Robert remembered the last conversation with Victoria in which he realized that she could help him a lot with the theme of emotional intelligence. "Besides, that skill would be very useful at work, to deal with Gerard and his colleagues. By the way, now that I think about it, you're advising me, Stephen!"

"Ha, ha, ha, ha!" Stephen couldn't contain a loud laugh. "You're right. In the end it will turn out that you are a better coach than me. Do you realize, Rob, that the answer was inside you?"

"Yeah, but surely, we won't end the session without you having advised me again. I bet you ten bucks that you advise me again." Robert winked at Stephen, and they both laughed.

"Done deal! I see that you understand that coaching is not advising, but actively listening to your interlocutor." After a pause, Stephen asked Robert the next question. "And how are you going to protect your family life when you are required to work overtime?"

"That is the part that scares me. I am afraid to refuse and jeopardize my job. Although, as I told you, Arty recently advised me to eliminate fear from the equation."

"Your friend Arthur is starting to seem very interesting to me, really. Indeed, decisions made with fear are not usually right. Will you let me leave the role of coach to serve as a counselor for a second?" Asked Stephen very seriously.

"You surprise me, Stephen. I thought that the coaches were not advisors and that they only listened," replied Robert with a wide smile and winking at Stephen. "Go ahead then, I'm on fire, and, by the way, I won the bet, and someone owes ten bucks to someone." He winked at Stephen again and they both laughed.

"Robert, have you ever heard of 'Agilism'?"

"I've heard something but, to be honest, I don't know what it is about," replied Robert with shame.

"'Agilism' is a trend that emerged in the '90s. They realized that software development required a lot of creativity and was surrounded by uncertainty. They also realized that, by treating programmers as slaves, the creativity and flexibility they needed were not achieved. Therefore, they invented a way to develop applications iteratively and incrementally, focusing on the individual, to treat them with respect and confidence. A constant and sustainable rhythm was sought that allowed the work to be carried out without burning out the team. I tell you this because, if you try to enter the Agile World, you'll be respected, and you won't have to work overtime. In fact, the team participates so much, and it is so committed that, in a few months, it becomes a high-performance team, and, with a high-performance team, twice as much work is carried out in half the time. But it requires having faith in the team and in the methodology, and trusting that the project will be successful. As your friend says, you have to remove fear from the equation."

"I can't believe it! There cannot be such an amazing movement!" exclaimed Robert enthusiastically. At that time, he also remembered Arthur's definition of faith and love, as self-induced states of autosuggestion. "By the way, and what is that idea that applications are developed iteratively and incrementally?"

"Very easy: the team works during an iteration, and something that works is delivered for the client; they look at it, and give us valuable feedback information. This way we know whether we're going in the right direction. If we were wrong, we'd learn from the mistakes and repeat the process for the next iteration. That is what iterative means. In each iteration the product functionalities are increased, so it isn't built all at once, but by increments. That is what incremental means. With client feedback you know that, in the end, you will give them what they really want."

"It has all the logic in the world. I can't believe I've been programming so many years, and I'd never heard anything about it. It is hard to believe it."

"Believe it because, in fact, I am, among other things, an expert coach in 'Agilism'. I offer my services to companies, to accompany them on their journey to 'Agilism'. Anyway, I remind you that to have an experience of ten years is not the same as to have repeated the same year ten times."

"It's true!" exclaimed Robert, who finally realized how little he learned in so many years. "I've just realized how mediocre I've been all these years."

"No, please, Robert! It has not been my intention to depress you. If you want, I can recommend you some books; you read them, and try to evangelize your boss with the subject. You can start with *Scrum for Non-Techies*, by a Spaniard, Antonio Montes Orozco, who explains the ultimate reason why "Agilism" is so powerful. In addition, it is a basic for both techies, like you, and for non-techies. If you understand why something works, it is easier for you to apply it well."

"Great, Stephen. I think you contribute much more as an advisor than as a coach," Robert said with a wide smile.

"HA, HA, HA!" laughed Stephen loudly.

Antonio Montes Orozco

"What strikes me is that the job of coach exists. So bad are we that we don't know how to ask ourselves the right questions, and that we need to pay for someone to listen to us?" Robert said suddenly.

"You're right. You've described it perfectly. In fact, in the most productive coaching sessions I've had, I haven't understood much: the client has left enthusiastic, and with a clear plan in mind. As they told themselves everything and answered the questions themselves, I couldn't understand much. We live in a world where people listen little to each other. Hence the concept of 'active listening', which is to put all our senses at our service, so as not to lose a single detail of what is being said, and thus understand everything as it is said. 'Active listening' would be linked to 'Emotional Intelligence'. It is very smart to listen carefully. For this, it is typical to paraphrase and ask: 'Is this what you've told me?' This way we make sure that we've understood our interlocutor. Once you internalize it, you get used to paying attention, and there's nothing left without understanding it firstly." Stephen's cell phone alarm suddenly sounded. "I'm so sorry, Rob, but I'm afraid the time is up."

"Well, here you are, a hundred and twenty bucks minus ten, so I give you a hundred and ten. It's been a pleasure: expensive, but a pleasure," said Robert sarcastically.

"Thanks a lot. You know where I am, so come back whenever you want. You've got a coach inside you, and you've done it perfectly. Come on, give me a hug." Stephen gave a hug to Robert, and they both said goodbye, satisfied with the session.

When Robert returned home, Victoria went out to meet him, eager to know how he'd done with the coach. Her husband was excited, and ideas were running through his head.

"How did it go, honey?" asked Victoria, very happy to talk to her husband.

"Well, I'm still processing it. It's been sensational, and Stephen, that's what the coach's name is, has broken the rules twice to act as an advisor, and tell me that there's a software movement called 'Agilism', in which programmers are respected, and work with quality. He's recommended me a book to learn what it's about. I'm going to read it right now."

"Great! Well, I'm really glad. And about sleeping, did he tell you anything?"

"Well, that's funny, I've told myself almost everything. I'll cut out reading at night, and I'll sleep eight hours. If I come home too late, I will also stop watching TV, and I will go to bed soon. In fact, he agrees with Arty that the best thing for us is talking. Watching TV prevents us from communicating. We'll watch something on the weekend. Then I won't make so many mistakes at work, and we will make better progress in the project. In addition, it'll be good for us as a couple. You'll see how you notice it in a few days," replied Robert, all in joy.

The first day Robert went to bed early, he didn't notice anything. It was obvious that the body does not recover easily from having been days without sleeping. But, on the fourth day, he began to notice a remarkable improvement. He was more optimistic, because now he had a plan: sleeping. He was also taking care of himself, since he had gone to do the blood tests. And, in a few days, he would go back to Dr. Serene's office, that strange doctor who prescribed reading books and going to coaches. In addition, Victoria, who saw him more awake and communicative, began to be livelier. Every afternoon they found a time to talk about this and that, as the occasions arose.

One day, Robert asked her, "Vicky, I've decided that I'll have faith, like you. Therefore, I'd like you to help me, since you're an expert and I'm a beginner. It will be good for me to exercise faith, since applying the new development methodologies implies an act of initial faith to trust the team, and a secondary one to trust the methodology itself."

"Really, Rob? But if you've never shown interest in religion."

"Yeah, but Arty told me that each one decides whether they want to have faith or whether they want to love someone, and that, therefore, love and faith are states of self-induced autosuggestion."

"Ha, ha, ha, ha, ha, ha!" laughed Victoria, surprised that she could suddenly share faith with her husband. "This Arty is blessed. He's done much good to this couple with his wise advice."

"Well, I'm at your disposal, teacher."

"As you accumulate books to read, come with me to church and you'll learn things. In addition, you'll discover how powerful the prayer made with faith is."

A lot to read. Starting with nutrition

Robert's books accumulated to read. He had four pending books and it seemed excessive to read several at once. As his life was going through a hard stage, he decided that the first thing was his health, both mental and physical, so he decided to start with the nutrition book that Dr. Serene recommended on the last visit. Then he would change the subject and start exploring the world of 'emotional intelligence', reading the book recommended by Coach Stephen. By the time he finished it, he would be eating healthy and could finish off the health issue, reading the first book the doctor sent him. Then, leading a healthy life with emotional abilities, he would study 'Agilism'.

He also remembered that a steady and sustainable pace had to be maintained, just as Stephen had told him. So every day he spent thirty minutes reading about nutrition. It was a sufficient rhythm to finish the book, and that allowed him to rest eight hours. He discovered that Dr. Serene was right: in society almost nothing is known about nutrition. People do not know what it is to eat healthy, and what the body needs to have all the vitamins and components it needs.

Another thing that shocked him was that diets in general were not advised; instead it was more important learning to eat correctly. Robert tended to gain weight easily, so he had already tried several of the most varied diets. As he did not really know how to eat healthy, after losing weight and abandoning the diet, he returned to his old habits, so he gained weight again, and gained even more weight than before. Therefore, the book advised against diets from the first page. In addition, many diets lacked a serious scientific basis and could even seriously harm health. Once again, he discovered that fear was the engine of many decisions, so certain fraudulent diets spread throughout society, based on people's fear of getting fat and suffering from cardiovascular disease. Eliminating the variable 'fear' from the equation, it was easy to realize what was scientific and truthful, and what was a pseudo-science that could put health at risk.

He discovered, for example, that there was no need to eat meat every meal. The amino acids needed to make proteins were stored in the liver, and used when they were required, so it was not necessary to have protein at lunch and dinner. In addition, he had read some scientific article about Alzheimer's and Parkinson's, and some suspected that they were related to excessive meat intake.

He also discovered that having vegetables was necessary, as well as legumes and fruit. Besides, there was the need to have vitamin C, which not only is used by the body to produce the collagen that heals wounds and to improve iron absorption, but that vitamin also contributes to the proper functioning of the immune system, which protects the body against diseases. To make sure he had the recommended daily fruit, he decided to have only fruit for breakfast, so he ate every day for breakfast an apple, an orange, and a banana. He discovered that it was more than enough to endure all morning until lunchtime. In addition, he made sure to maintain an acceptable level of vitamins provided by the fruit. He remembered the famous saying: "An apple a day, keeps the doctor away." As the seasonal fruit came, he would adapt to the different seasons so that it'd be cheaper.

Then he also discovered the trick of mixing legumes with cereals to add protein because, among the amino acids provided by the legumes, and the amino acids provided by cereals, in the end he had all the necessary amino acids for his body to make proteins. In this way he could reduce the intake of meat and increase that of vegetables. So he decided to take a Tupperware to work and eat a few days broccoli, other legumes (chickpeas, lentils, beans, etc.), other spinach, other brown rice, etc. On the days he took only legumes or vegetables, he had protein for dinner at home: beef or chicken. He couldn't stop eating meat, as he would run out of vitamin B12, and this was important to keep neurons and red blood cells healthy. In addition, the lack of B12 could cause a rare type of anemia that caused fatigue and weakness, which was just what Robert wanted to recover from.

The first day he took a Tupperware with broccoli to work, he had to endure the complaints of his companions, since the broccoli smelled really bad and left a stink throughout the coffee room. But it was very healthy and, once a week, it wasn't that bad.

"Can't you bring a good hamburger, like any normal guy?" asked William, one of the programmers who got along better with Robert. "If it smells that bad, imagine what it can do to your body."

"Come on Bill, it's hard for me to eat healthy. Don't make it so difficult for me," replied Robert, resigning himself and taking out all his patience.

"You are too young to be in a mid-life crisis."

"Bill, I really appreciate you, so respect me, please. And you also tend to be overweight, so it wouldn't hurt you to follow my example."

"Sure, and look how healthy I look."

"No one is a prophet in their land, of course," said Robert with resignation."

"Ha, ha, ha, ha!" William ended up laughing. "By the way, there 'The Exterminator of Programmers' comes, our well-known Carol." Caroline was also a project manager, just like

Gerard. And, like him, she also had her team demotivated and exhausted.

"What's up, guys, it seemed as if you were laughing at me, weren't you?" asked Caroline with authority. "This week I've lost two programmers, and I am liable to take out my anger on you."

"Not at all," replied William. "Remind me when you form a new team, to go on vacation and avoid being chosen.

"Very funny, Bill." Caroline glared at him.

"Come on, Bill, let's leave Carol in peace," commented Robert in a whisper.

Following the science articles, Robert remembered that colon cancer was linked to the lack of fiber intake. There were several types of colon cancer, and there were several types of fiber: a cancer was caused by the absence of cereal fiber in the diet; and the other colon cancer was caused by the absence of fiber from fruits and vegetables (legumes, for example) in the diet.

He also discovered that many people did not know that rice and corn were also cereals. One day, he put a test on Victoria.

"Vicky, I'm seeing spots with the second book that Dr. Serene recommended me. By the way, I discovered a very interesting fact: could you tell me the cereals you know?"

"Of course. Wheat, barley, rye, and oats are cereals."

"You are missing two very important ones, honey."

"Well, now I can't figure it out."

"Corn and rice are cereals too."

"Come on, I didn't know!" replied Victoria surprised.

In a natural way, Robert began to lose weight. In addition, the cold symptoms disappeared, so he began to feel very good. It seemed that having the vitamin C intake assured helped him to be in good health. It is also true that he kept on eating excessively, like eating ribs every time he went out to dinner with Victoria on the weekend. But as the rest of the days he ate very healthy, his body did not protest and he continued losing weight and improving.

Now it was time to change the subject.

The 'Emotional Intelligence'

Once Robert focused his eating habits, he began to read the book on 'Emotional Intelligence' that the coach Stephen had recommended.

"Vicky, I have discovered that Emotional Intelligence is learned mostly at home, during the childhood, and that it is part of the social structure within the family. Now I understand why you have so much Emotional Intelligence. Only by observing your father you can tell that you have inherited it from him. I was not so lucky."

Antonio Montes Orozco

"Well, I love you, so your parents had to have done something good. Besides, your mother and I get along very well.

"The pity is that you couldn't meet my father; you would've liked him very much. Continuing with the theme of Emotional Intelligence, I still remember the time I visited the Marketing Department, and they asked me about my opinion of that department. Instead of focusing on how well-organized marketing campaigns were, and highlighting what I liked, I told them that I preferred my IT Department. I acted like a fool, really. There you can see the little Emotional Intelligence that I've happened to have."

"Rob, don't beat yourself with that. Focus on that you have finally realized your error, and that, from now on, you will evaluate the situations in a more constructive way."

"I know, but now I've realized, suddenly, the dumb ass you've had to endure all these years. I am ashamed, really."

"Come here, my fool." Vicky hugged him and they both laughed.

But Robert really didn't stay calm, because he was the way he was, and he did not know how to change. He had the tendency to be impulsive, and often had to regret what he said. So one day he decided to meet his friend Arthur to talk about it.

"How are you doing, student?" asked Arthur.

"Well, studying hard, but I see that studying theory, and then seeing that things cannot be changed, disappoints me a lot. I am as I am. This Emotional Intelligence is not for me."

"No, Rob! Don't fall into the trap of labeling yourself and throwing in the towel!" Arthur jumped like a spring. "The human being is capable to decide how they want to be! Trends can be changed, and we can reinvent ourselves to be as we please!" explained Arthur, calmer.

"Come on! I am like this! Why fighting against my nature?"

"Robert, this is a great secret that I share with you. We can be as we please. If you want to be patient, you can generate patience. If you want to practice 'active listening', you can do it. If you want to empathize with others and understand their fears and what moves them, you can do it. Everything is a matter of will and practice. Like when you learn to play the guitar: you practice until your fingers bleed, as Angus Young said, and, when they bleed, you keep on practicing."

"I'm glad you mention 'active listening'. That's what Stephen, the coach, told me. Okay, I will attempt to do this. I'll end up exhausted, because it'll involve being constantly aware of what I answer, aware of how I listen, and aware of what I am understanding: it'll be exhausting. By the way, I liked your reference to Angus Young. Your musical tastes are notable." Robert winked at Arthur.

Antonio Montes Orozco

"Ha, ha, ha!" laughed Arthur. "Yeah, Rob, but when you get it, it will come out without thinking. Come on, give me a hug. You are a machine, and you will succeed."

Both hugged and said goodbye. The truth is that the idea of being the owner of your way of being was a very novel idea to Robert. Everything resided in willpower. If it was so easy and so cool, why did most people tend not to fight and justify themselves? Was it something as silly as being too lazy to fight, and that it involved an effort? Besides, it required a lot of humility to recognize that you had a lack, and begin learning and improving. It was clear that pride prevented us from reaching our full potential.

But Robert saw value in getting Emotional Intelligence, so he started to get it. He also discovered in other people the Emotional Intelligence. Sometimes he was dumbfounded in the parks, seeing mothers with their children: it was amazing the patience they had, and how they were able to reason with them, avoiding direct confrontation and bringing their attention to other things. For the first time, Robert found himself thinking of forming a family. Everything came in life, but tranquility and balance were needed, and the periods of work stress didn't help at all. As soon as this period of stress was over, he would propose Victoria that they form a family.

He also began to empathize with his colleagues at work, and discovered the fears that ate them inside: fear of losing their job, fear of aging, fear of being left alone, fear of getting ill. Fear clouded our intellect, and made us aggressive and treat our partners badly. As Arthur said, "We had to eliminate fear from the equation" so we can make the decisions much better.

The glucose cycle

After reading the book of nutrition and the book on emotional intelligence, Robert began the penultimate book in the series, the one that talked about the glucose cycle in human beings.

Now he understood what Dr. Serene talked about. The energy consumed by the brain and muscles is glucose. A typical form of glucose is sugar, present in so many foods and drinks. What surprised Robert the most was that the refined wheat from the bread, and the mass of the pizzas, were practically all glucose. That meant that, by eating white bread, whether it was at lunch or in the form of pizza, we were really putting a glucose peak in our bodies. To prevent it from accumulating in the blood, it is important to remove this glucose from the body, either with strong intellectual activity or with physical exercise. If the glucose remained in the blood and did not leave, there was a risk of hyperglycemia; that is, an excess of glucose in the blood, which could lead to kidney failure, eye damage, or even damage to cardiovascular system and other internal organs. But, fortunately, the body has a way to eliminate excess glucose, and it consists of producing insulin through the pancreas. Insulin introduces glucose into the cells, so that they could eliminate it. The problem comes when, due to bad eating habits, people spend the day having sugar, white bread, white rice, and pizzas made from refined wheat. With each of these intakes, a glucose peak is produced that endangers health, so the body was forced to produce insulin throughout the whole day. After a few years, the pancreas ends up so depleted that it stops working, so the dreaded type 2 diabetes mellitus appears. It could also happen that the cells became resistant to insulin, so our pancreas entered a cycle where it produced insulin to eliminate glucose, but, since the cells were resistant to insulin, glucose was not eliminated, so it continued to produce more insulin. This cause also leads to type 2 diabetes mellitus.

The solution to this situation is to take glucose accompanied by fiber, thus reducing the glucose peak, since the fiber makes an amalgam with the glucose in the stomach, gradually releasing glucose, thus giving the brain and muscles more time to absorb it. Therefore, you have to remove the sugar from coffees, and have whole grains: whole wheat bread, brown rice, whole-grain pizza dough, or have vegetable fiber and vegetables when refined wheat flour or refined rice are consumed. In this way, the stress on the pancreas is stopped and the risk of suffering from type 2 diabetes mellitus is reduced. If it is so clear that refining cereals do give nothing but problems, Robert did not understand how this practice was so widespread in our society.

"Vicky, the first book that Dr. Serene prescribed for me is great. I have learned that cereals contain a lot of energy in the form of glucose, apart from fiber, amino acids, and vitamins. All this, as long as we have them whole and not refined. I do not understand why our society refines cereals, if it is precisely in the fiber where vitamins and proteins are found. In addition, cereal fiber is necessary to avoid a type of colon cancer."

"But Rob, white bread is much tastier. Brown bread is very coarse."

"I know, Vicky, but why putting a peak of glucose to the body, and then taking away the wheat proteins, vitamins, and fiber? I do not get it. Who came up with that absurd idea?"

"In the cooking course I attended last year they explained that white bread was consumed by the upper social classes, as it was finer and less coarse than unrefined bread. In the eighteenth century is when the techniques of milling cereals in flour were improved, and that is when the use of white bread was extended, since the price of bread fell, and people were willing to try the delicacy of the most favored social groups."

"Your memory surprises me, Vicky. Anyway, the funny thing is that now the cheap thing is refined bread, and the expensive one is whole wheat bread. I don't understand that mania that humanity has to destroy itself."

"Rob, and what are you going to do, stop having bread?"

"No, but I will combine its intake with fiber intake."

"I believe that the balance is in moderation. My grandmother has eaten bread all her life, and look at her how healthy she is with her bread, and she is ninety-four years old. I don't think you become diabetic for having some bread."

"You're right, Vicky. But admit that I was going to become diabetic, because I had the muffin in the morning, then the coffees filled with sugar, then I ate white rice with white bread, following the afternoon with some coffee with sugar, and finishing with another muffin during the dinner, where I had white bread, of course."

"Okay, yeah, you haven't been moderate at all. Bless this doctor and the books he has recommended to you."

Months passed and, in general, Robert kept coming home late. At least now he empathized with his companions and, returning home daily, dedicated to really communicating with Victoria, so he rediscovered his wife. It was clear that television cut off communication, so he could not base leisure and rest on watching series.

All that remained was to learn about 'Agilism'. He'd heard of Scrum: it was a software development framework, but he didn't know exactly what it involved, or why it was becoming so famous. So he started reading the book Stephen had recommended.

The world of 'Agilism'

In the following days, Robert devoted himself to studying the book Stephen recommended about the world of 'Agilism' and its practices: *Scrum for Non-Techies*. He discovered that, in the XP development methodology, an acronym for 'Extreme Programming', work was limited to forty hours per week. The entire Agile movement was impregnated with trusting the workers, giving them the power to decide how to do things, and maintaining an environment of mutual respect, without lies or distrust. He also discovered that everything revolved around the principle of Stephen Covey that coach Stephen had told him, and that stated: 'Without involvement, there is no commitment'.

Comparing the trust in human being that Agilism had, with the general distrust that was felt in companies, it was clear that an act of faith in Agilism was required to deliver power and trust to a team.

The Scrum methodology made a lot of sense. As was done with the classical methodology, a complete list of tasks is created. The difference is that the classic tasks could be abstract things that did not add any value to the client, such as "connect to the database". Agilism focuses on the value that was generated in the client, to be able to return the investment, so that the tasks are of the form: "Show the client their bank accounts", for example. That task that added value already involved connecting to the database, but what brought value in itself was to show to the client their bank accounts, not that the system connected to a database. That way of partitioning the work kept the team closer to the client, and with their feet on the ground.

Antonio Montes Orozco

Then there was another facet of Agilism that Robert loved, and it was to assume that the client did not know what they wanted, and that they had a hard time communicating it, so they had to be helped to clarify ideas. For this, a few functionalities were made that would provide value and worked, so that the result was shown to the client, they clarified ideas and gave feedback, so in the end the team ended up delivering what the client really wanted. This caused the product to be built iteratively, functionality after functionality. In Scrum, each iteration is called *a Sprint*.

As trust is given to the team and it is allowed to be involved in the decisions, it is fully committed, and, in a few months, it becomes a high-performance team that got double the work in half the time. This eliminates overtime and reinforces optimism in the team, as they are happy and can rest in the afternoon.

All the team members fight to get work done, and all of them contribute value. To reinforce the team idea, a synchronization meeting is held every day. This meeting is quick and used to be done standing up so that the team does not relax, and the meeting finishes quickly. Each and every team member contributes, commenting on what they did the previous day, what problems they faced, and what they would do that same day. In this way they synchronized every day and everyone knows how the project is going, thus achieving a great team awareness and focusing on the work to the fullest.

Robert was excited. So many years suffering from disrespect at companies, and there were islands where there were happy programmers! Working overtime was counterproductive, it was clear: fatigue increased, and this led to more mistakes at work. The evil had spread throughout the team, so they worked carelessly, and then they had to invest time in fixing what they had done wrong in that state of extreme tiredness. In addition, as they weren't fully committed with the project, they projected all the tension onto the project manager, in this case Gerard, who was practically alone with an exhausted team that worked without creativity, without adding value, and making many mistakes.

That curse had to be broken. They had to rest, but Robert did not see how to talk to Gerard about this issue. His boss wasn't an 'agilist' and could be seized by fear, so he would surely see it as an attempt to boycott the project.

Apart from that, the Agilism approach was to adapt to change, considering change as something inherent in the world around us. It was based on the fact that it was impossible to describe an entire software project from the beginning, because clients never knew exactly what they wanted. Therefore, the primary qualities of the project were established, which would be the ones with the highest return on investment, so that the team would always work on what brought more value to business, thus avoiding the loss of time and money. The progress in the product would be shown iteratively, so the final product would be built based on increments. Each increment would add more value to the final product, and the client would always give their assessment of what was delivered, to adapt the result to their wishes, since, as the process progressed, the client would know what they wanted as the final product.

Robert began to notice that the weeks of intense study he was carrying out were giving him a clear vision. One day, he met Caroline in the break room. She was railing against the lack of coordination within her team.

"But did nobody know that today we were performing the monthly reload of the database, and that it wasn't a good day to touch it?" asked Caroline bitterly.

"Caroline, may I tell you something?" asked Robert to Caroline.

"Yeah, tell me. But quickly; we have to fix a mistake the team has made."

"I haven't been able to avoid hearing you, and I propose that you have a synchronization meeting within the team every day. In this way, you will know what's important, you'll focus your efforts, and you'll know perfectly what each one is working on. This way you will avoid stepping on each other's work. How about having a brief meeting every day, early in the morning, with the whole team, where each one answers these three questions: What did I do yesterday? What problems did I encounter? And the last one: What am I going to do today? This way you all will be synchronized. And, if there were problems, surely a colleague would have the solution to solve the task. Of course, to avoid wasting time, it is important that the meeting be every day at the same time, and in the same place, to create a routine. Oh, and it's important that there are no chairs, and that all the team members are standing, so that they do not relax and you are able to synchronize in fifteen minutes maximum. What do you think about it?" asked Robert finally.

"All right, as Gerard says, I buy you the idea," replied Caroline, smiling.

"You're very smart, Carol, you're quick to understand. Tell me next week how you're doing."

The following week, Robert asked Caroline, one day when he found her in the break room.

"How are you doing? How about those synchronization meetings?"

"Very good, really. We haven't screwed up again, and now everyone knows what to do every day, without stepping on each other's work. The other day I was surprised by the team, because I was late, talking to Gerard, and, when I arrived, the team was already having the daily meeting, and they were synchronizing without me!"

"Congratulations, Carol! That is the property of a self-organized team: it works alone without the bosses having to hold the reins. How did you get it in just one week?"

"Tricks of an experienced project manager. I leave them to do as they pleased, because they are empowered, and, apart from that, they've been working together for a long time. They quickly saw value in the synchronization meeting, so they received it with enthusiasm. But still things aren't going as well as they could. They make many mistakes, and I feel they are stuck."

"What are they dedicating their efforts to?"

"Well, to the plan we made at the beginning of the project. We are following the established order."

"Have you shown anything to the client? What criteria are you following to prioritize the tasks?"

"Well, we followed the document of the offer, and we took out the tasks from there. At the end of the development we will test and deliver it to the client."

"Carol, of all the projects you have done, how many were well specified? What's more, how many were delivered and were just what the client had asked for?"

"Don't know, to tell you the truth. In all of them I've suffered a lot. But I've managed to deliver all of them."

"I offer you the following: every day we dedicate a few minutes to your list of tasks, and group them into functionalities that add value. After finishing each functionality, we show it working to the client, so that they decide whether they like it or not; thus they can give us their feedback. Would you sign up?"

"Would you do that for me? Has the cauliflower melted your brain?"

"Okay, it smells badly, but it's very healthy, and I've never felt better. Does it make you happy then?"

"All right, we'll try it," replied Caroline, with a breath of hope for the first time in a long time.

Caroline and Robert shook hands. Robert was surprised that everything had been so easy. Certainly, there were people who had great intuition, and Caroline was one of them. If Caroline's support was won, it would be very easy to convince Gerard.

During the following days, Robert stayed with Caroline in a meeting room, where they spent twenty minutes each day refining the list of tasks. They realized about the dependencies that there were, and that it was difficult to group the tasks by functionalities that added value. But, after a week, they had it. It had cost, but the result looked very good.

"Shock those five, Carol!" They high fived, very satisfied. "Now it is the turn of your team to focus on the first functionality, because we've seen that it's the one that gives most value to the client. And remember, fight to ensure that when your team finishes, it shows the result to the client, so they give you feedback on what you have shown them. And keep on with the daily sync meetings. Remember that, in those meetings, they are the ones that synchronize with each other, and that it is not a report meeting to you."

"But where did you get these ideas?" asked Caroline with intrigue.

"From a very good book that a friend recommended. Its name is *Scrum for Non-Techies*. It's about a new way of working called Agile, where high-performance teams are formed that work very well together, and where the whole focus is placed on adding value to the client and listening to the feedback they provide when something is delivered to them. Everything is based on the principle that states that, 'Without involvement, there is no commitment'. You have to let your team participate in decisions, so that they really commit to the project."

"Have you talked to Gerard?"

"No, I haven't. But, if you see it makes sense, as you are the project manager, you can adopt these practices and, when we see that it works, we can pose them to Gerard."

"All right, we try it with the first functionality, and we'll see. I'm very grateful to you, really."

"Great, Caroline."

The following week, Robert met Caroline again in the coffee office:

"How's it going, Carol?"

"Well, very good. We are all focused on this delivery, and being the most valuable team, we are looking forward to seeing the client's reaction when they receive it."

"And the environment within the team?"

"Very good, and they are delighted to work like this, with clear objectives and synchronizing daily."

"And you, how do you see yourself? What do you do?"

"Well, I don't stop, because, all day, I'm looking for ways to facilitate their job. I've also started reading the book and it's clarifying my ideas a lot. I've discovered why they used to dislike me so much before. But now, we all see that this's going to be fine and we focus on providing value. In addition, the fear of every project manager is that team members stop for lack of work. As we have planned the work, I know that, when they finish with one task, they'll get the next one, so the efficiency of the team increases, and I'm less stressed. I could even get ill, or go on vacation, and I'd know that the project would continue by itself."

"These months I've also learned to eliminate fear from the equation, to have a clear mind and without pressure, and thus make better decisions," commented Robert. "Before your change, were you afraid of something?"

"Well, now that you mention it, you're right!" answers Caroline seeing the light for the first time. "I was afraid of not delivering the project on time, or that I had many mistakes, or, as I told you before, that the team members stopped. I used to blame the team for my fears, and treated them harshly. That's why they burned out and left the company, making the situation even worse. Now that I'm not afraid, I am confident that everything will be fine. They're noticing it. Do you know that the other day they told me that I was like their mother? I liked that. It shows that there is love."

"You surprise me, Carol. You've seen it clear. I've needed books and hours to change, and you've seen it immediately. Don't forget to tell me the reaction of the client when you show them something that works. You'll see how important their feedback is."

"Count on it, Rob. I feel like your guinea pig. I hope you are sure of what you advise."

"Don't worry. Eliminate fear from the equation, and you'll realize that all this makes a lot of sense, and that it's the way to go." Robert winked at Caroline, and they both laughed. "By the way, it's amazing how we can change, and how we can be as we want to be. My friend Arthur told me that we could change, but, until you see it, it's hard to believe it."

"Well, now that you mention, it's true. Look at me: now they even appreciate me. Oh, and now I am a mother to them." Caroline laughed and tapped Robert on the shoulder. "And you're no longer as uncouth as you used to be, when you used to employ such a rough tone that you scared people." Robert couldn't avoid a loud laugh, remembering how asinine he'd been all those years.

After obtaining the support of Caroline, Robert was encouraged to keep putting into practice what he'd learned. He was still exhausted, and there were two clear options, or to evangelize with the new methodology to the team he belonged to, or to go to another company where they used that methodology. Robert was in a bind because, with the first option, he would have to deal with Gerard, although Caroline would support him; and, with the second, he would have to spend time looking for another job, and time was what he didn't have. In addition, he wasn't very interested in losing the seniority he had in his current company.

Robert thought of Stephen's words when he told him that the answer was within him. What if he tried to do an auto-coaching session? By asking himself the right questions, he could come up with the solution. Applying GROW, he would start with the 'G', that is, the goals: his objectives were to be treated more humanely at work, avoiding overtime, and that the project worked out well. Followed by 'R', the reality was that, if they stopped making so many mistakes, and stopped working overtime, the project would end well, and they would have a decent quality of life. Then he applied the 'O', and the options were two: changing to another company or evangelizing Gerard. And finally came the million-dollar question, that is, the 'W': how would he get the project to end well and have a decent quality of life? The answer was clear: evangelizing the team!

Robert suddenly felt infinite thanks to Stephen's wise teachings. He was afraid that he had saved $120 with his auto-coaching session, but he couldn't be paying that money every time he had to make a decision, and especially now that Victoria didn't work.

"Vicky, I know what I'm going to do!" Robert climbed the stairs of the house with enthusiasm; He needed to tell his wife everything.

"Ha, ha, ha!" laughed Victoria when she saw that her husband was so excited. "But what's wrong with you, honey?"

"Well, I've encountered the best coach in the city and he's taught me very well the procedure of asking myself the right questions, so I've done an auto-coaching session, and I already know what I'm going to do in order not to suffer more overtime: I'm going to evangelize the guys in the office to adopt 'Agilism'!"

"But if you're already doing it with Caroline? Didn't you tell me the other day that she was very excited about the new methodology?"

"Yeah, it's true. But that has come naturally. What I'm thinking now is commenting about it to Gerard, and making the change officially."

"And, now that you mention it, have you thought about how he's going to take it?" asked Victoria with curiosity.

"I hope well. I will have to use a lot of tact, but I am clear that you are my priority, and that overtime is killing our marriage. So, either Gerard understands, or I will look for a company where they are interested in following the philosophy of 'Agilism'. Also, as I've been evangelizing Carol in the new way of working these weeks, she'll be a great support to convince Gerard."

"Go ahead, Rob. I am very proud of you. Start that revolution now. And remember to 'remove fear from the equation', as Arty told you.

Robert and Victoria hugged each other. Life has turned them around, and now they feel they have control of their destiny.

Chapter 3: The Revolution

Chatting with Gerard

After the weekend, Robert was looking forward to going to work, because the next Monday he would talk to Gerard. He had been studying what Agilism was for many weeks, and now he was sure that it was a framework that would come in handy for his company, and that would get them out of trouble. But inertia cannot be broken easily, and the first thing he had to get was to attract Gerard's attention.

"Good morning, Gerard. Later, when you have a while and are in the mood to listen, I'd like to talk to you about an idea I have."

"Good morning, Rob. At noon I have a meeting, and it'll last half an hour, so, if you agree, I'll meet you at about twelve thirty."

"That sounds great. At twelve thirty then."

Robert was very nervous, because he was going to turn his entire employment status upside down. He was afraid that Gerard would feel threatened by the new idea of Agilism, and see him as an enemy. He had to deal with the change very tactfully. But, as Arthur said, he had to eliminate fear from the equation. Besides, Caroline would support him.

He programmed in the morning solving some bugs that were in the code. Time flew by, and soon twelve thirty arrived. He got up from his seat and headed to Gerard's desk, where he was waiting.

"Hi, Gerard. Is now a good time for you?"

"Yeah, come on, shoot."

"Look, lately, we have entered a crunch of work that has us all exhausted. As we arrive home late, we refuse to spend the day without having some down time, and we have down time at the expense of our sleep, so we sleep less and less, and come here in the morning completely exhausted. That exhaustion leads us to make mistakes. These mistakes worsen the situation and load us with more work, so the project keeps on being delayed. All this without mention that extreme fatigue causes us to fall ill, so colleagues go sick by waves, and stop coming to the office, thus causing more delay in the project. Therefore, I think that, in order to save the project, we have to get out of this dynamic of extreme fatigue, and stop making so many mistakes. By making fewer mistakes or even eliminating them, confidence in the deadlines would return and we would begin to be predictable, and keep a steady and sustainable pace. I've been studying for weeks a new movement called 'Agilism', which I think is the solution to our current problems. Would you want me to explain what it is about?"

"Rob, I'm also very tired and I have a lot of pressure on my shoulders. But for now, what you tell me doesn't seem bad at all. Explain to me what Agilism is about. I am very tired, and the first thing that comes to my mind is to come in tracksuit and start doing gymnastics in the office."

"Ha, ha, ha, ha! No man!" laughed Robert loudly. "Agilism is a movement that began in the nineties. It started with people who suffered the same situation we are suffering now: projects that were twisted, and exhausting workdays that burned programmers out. These gurus focused on creating high-performance teams that worked very well together: like a perfectly oiled clockwork mechanism. The software they produced was of high quality and contained very few bugs, and they used to show it to the client in each delivery. Incorporating the client into the process had the advantage that they clarified ideas, and made a concrete idea of what they wanted so, in the end, they ended up delivering what the client really wanted. In addition, development teams were obsessed with not wasting a single minute of their time, so they eliminated any task that was not productive and did not have a direct translation on the return of investment. How does what I'm telling sound to you, Gerard?"

"Well, it is sounding very good to me, because you are talking about high-performance teams and return of investment, and that, from the point of view of a project manager like me, sounds very interesting."

"These gurus also had a lot of human psychology. They realized that we are tremendously visual, so they put the tasks on post-its placed on public boards, so that every morning a team meeting was held, in front of the task boards, to comment on that day's schedule, and make all aware of the work that had to be done. Those were short meetings, so as not to waste time, that involved everyone's participation. I have also discovered a principle that says, 'Without involvement there is no commitment'. By getting the entire team to participate in the decisions, everyone's commitment to the project is achieved. That's where the strength of Agile methodologies resides."

"May I interrupt you, Rob?" asked Gerard, who was beginning to show interest.

"Of course, Gerard. Go ahead, please."

"As project manager, I am asked for metrics to evaluate the progress of the project. How does that match with what you propose to me?" asked Gerard quite honestly.

"Well, these methodologies have a lot to do with trusting the team, so the best way to see how the project is going is with the delivery of software that works and that adds, delivery to delivery, functionality that increases value and returns part of the investment."

"Sorry to tell you, Rob, that I have to deliver progress reports and performance metrics. So this new methodology is not compatible with the real situation."

"As you say, I buy your claim. It occurs to me to take, from this new methodology, whatever serves us and is compatible with our reality. How about creating a high-performance team and an environment where trust prevails? The team, being high-performance and being immersed in an environment of trust, will do twice as much work in half the time. Would you buy me that idea, as you say?"

"Yeah, Rob. We have nothing to lose, and, up against a wall, we would continue to carry out the projects according to the protocols that have been established."

"Well, I propose to talk to the teammates, explain it to them, and start with this as soon as possible. I know that currently the project already has all the tasks prepared, but I'd like to select those that provide more value, and focus on deliveries every two weeks; for example, to be able to give the client something that works and adds value. Of course, it is clear that the project manager is you, and that I, at no time, intend to usurp that position. I would be a mere facilitator to achieve our goal, which is to finish the project successfully, and with congratulations from the client. That kind of servant leadership, where the team leader is a team facilitator, is typical of 'Agilism'. There are no bosses. You would play the role of 'Product Owner', so it would be your responsibility to decide the 'what'. The development team would be empowered and they would decide the 'how'."

"Sorry, I don't follow you," interrupted Gerard. "What is that that the team would be 'empowered'?"

"They are the ones who work, then they are the ones who decide. You will tell them the 'what', but they will decide the 'how'. Empowering a team requires a lot of faith in the methodology because, if they say no, it means no, and you have to abide by it."

"It makes sense." At that moment Gerard was silent, as if in ecstasy. After a moment of silence, he left his lethargy. "I buy you the idea, Rob!" said Gerard enthusiastically.

Both project manager and programmer shook hands and left the room very satisfied, because the meeting had been very fruitful, and they had reached a very healthy agreement.

Robert was admired. Applying the technique of coaching with himself, he had reached an action plan, had set it in motion, and now he began to see its fruits. He was surprised with Gerard, as he expected more resistance to change, but, in the end, Gerard was very receptive to the new idea. He was looking forward to talking with the guys, to see what they thought.

Chatting with the team

The meeting took place a few days later. Robert gathered the team in the morning, in a quiet room, and deliberately removed the chairs, forcing them to stand, and preventing them from relaxing. It had to be a brief meeting so that the guys didn't get nervous about 'wasting time', given the stress situation they were going through.

"Good morning, team. I've gathered you here and standing, to have a brief chat with you," said Robert.

"What do you mean, 'team', talking to us as if you were the project manager?" snapped Caroline, who had entered the room unexpectedly. Robert didn't expect her, because she didn't belong to Gerard's team. But Robert realized that Caroline was joking with him and followed her joke.

"Okay, well. Good morning, employees of this company that produces software," replied Robert.

"Come on, tell us what's up," said William, Robert's friend.

"I have gathered you here to denounce that we cannot continue like this. We are exhausted from working so many hours without stopping. We have no life outside these walls, and that is destroying us inside."

"That's true, that's true," murmured the employees.

"By the way, I've been studying these weeks, and I have discovered another, more efficient way of working, which has to do with a movement called 'Agilism'."

"What have you been smoking, Rob?" asked William sarcastically.

"Studying 'Agilism' I've seen the light, and I've understood why we are all overweight, grumpy, and unhealthy."

Antonio Montes Orozco

"In the end, did you realize that annoying us with Broccoli was not good?" snapped Caroline.

"Very funny, Carol. Yes, I apologize publicly for stifling you with broccoli. And now, seriously, let me tell you without interruptions," replied Robert calmly. "Look how we act in this company: a client comes and wants us to develop a software application. They give us an idea of what they want. Here the first problem begins, and it is that clients do not know what they want! In addition, they are very bad at specifying requirements for a software engineer to understand. That is a dogma that you should internalize. How many of you have ever encountered a well-defined new project from the beginning? Come on, I want to see those hands raised!"

No one was able to raise their hands, since the truth was that the requirements were never complete, and the teams suffered greatly until they managed to get the projects on track

"So we agree with this point," continued Robert. "And how do you get the client to clarify ideas, and learn how to tell us what they want? Well, very easy, trying to give them something that has minimal functionality, so that they try it, look at it and help them clarify ideas. Therefore, instead of developing the entire project, the most logical thing is to develop a bit that brings value, show it to the client, and wait for their feedback with comments. Applying this iterative procedure, in the end we will deliver something that is exactly what they wanted."

"It makes sense," says William.

Antonio Montes Orozco

"More than that. Rob and I have been with this for weeks, and I assure you it works. Here are some of my guys, and they can confirm it," says Caroline, to everyone's amazement, as they didn't expect that she supported Robert.

"Thanks a lot, Carol," replied Robert.

"But wait. Has anyone seen a client who is interested in development?" asked William.

"Good point, Bill," replied Robert. "We have to evangelize the clients in the new methodology and make them see that, with 'Agilism', their interests and ours will be the same; that is, that our clients are enriched, and that they can adapt to Market changes."

"It seems it has given you a streak of faith, Rob, but I support you one hundred percent," said Carol sarcastically, while giggles were heard around the room.

"Thanks a lot, Carol. Well, partly yes. In the end, it is a matter of faith. Faith is nothing more than believing in what we do not see. It's an act of self-induced autosuggestion. It doesn't matter that Jesus existed, that there is undeniable evidence that he died crucified, and that there are numerous witnesses of his resurrection: in the end, we have to want to have faith. That is, we have to tell ourselves to have it, and for that we have to convince ourselves of it. It doesn't matter if I come here and tell you that; if we treat people with respect, they will perform better, and that, if we work with the mindset of adding value, we will bring more benefits to the client, and we will all win.

Antonio Montes Orozco

In the end you have to self-induce yourself to autosuggest that 'Agilism' will lead us to success. It is an act of faith."

"Colleagues, as project manager I tell you that I believe in this new framework!" exclaimed Caroline. "I imagine that you'll have already spoken with my team members, and that they'll have already told you about the turnaround that our project has taken. We no longer do overtime, and we know that we will deliver to the client a project well finished and adjusted to their needs."

"Yes, Mom!" Several voices shouted in the back of the room.

"And you'll wonder how Carol has managed it," added Robert. "We have worked in two directions: the first one has been to empower the team to make decisions, and the second one has been to reorganize the work to devote our efforts, at all times, only to what brings more value, then showing the result to the client, in order for them to give us their feedback with their appreciations about what has been delivered. With this we have managed to form a high-performance team that is happy, and not wasting any minute of our time in bureaucracy nor in tasks that do not add value. We assume that people are willing to promote and accept more and more responsibility. In the end everyone seeks self-actualization, and, as long as that is not understood from management, they will have a bunch of exhausted programmers that are under-committed, and with no creativity."

Antonio Montes Orozco

"There, that's spot on!" was heard among the rows of programmers.

"Guys!" snapped Robert, raising his voice. "Has the slavery returned? Don't we have the right to live a dignified life? Why are we wasting the talent and intelligence God has given us with mediocre methodologies that are useless? Do you want to miss your children? Do you want to end your marriages?"

"NO!" they shouted all at once, including Caroline.

"Well then, what are you waiting for? Embrace 'Agilism' and you will be free!"

"YES!" they shrieked, all at once.

"Well, we start right now. I'm having a meeting with Gerard, and we'll do the same as Carol and I did." Robert began to organize the revolution. "I will assume the role of 'Scrum Master', who is the team facilitator, and I will facilitate your work, so that nothing stops you. And, of course, it's forbidden to work overtime. And you'll see how, in a short time, we will form a high-performance team that will successfully finish any project that is put in front of it.

"Have you talked to Gerard about this?" interrupted William.

"Yeah, I've got his approval. I've already explained him what 'Agilism' consists of, and he sees value in it. Believe me, in the end, we will wonder why we hadn't discovered it before, and it'll make us angry to have suffered so much."

All programmers returned, very impressed, to their desks. It seemed surreal how the meeting developed. They had a feeling between euphoria and disbelief. In general, they were all exhausted, and seeing the light at the end of the tunnel scared them, in case it was be a mirage. Robert was known by everyone, and they were aware of the change he suffered in recent weeks: both his home-made veggie-based meals, which left a stinky smell in the break room, as well as his change in attitude, when he used to be a bit clumsy. Now they found a leader with very clear ideas and able to drag the masses.

They saw the same change in Caroline, who now treated her team with love and became their 'mother'.

Change begins

That same day everyone went home on time. The next day they all looked better, because sleeping eight hours had left them as new.

Gerard and Robert locked themselves in a meeting room to set up the 'Product Backlog', which is the name that the list of tasks receive in 'Agilism'. They managed to divide all the work into tasks that added value as themselves, and that also could be completed in a two-week iteration. Among all of them, they chose the most important to give the client, as soon as possible, the 'minimum viable product', something that they could touch and judge, to clarify ideas and give their valuable feedback.

The team members eliminated habits that made them less productive, such as having a lot of coffees, unnecessarily extending the breaks, or spending too much time having lunch, all caused by knowing that they were going to spend many hours at the workplace. Since they now knew that they were going to be at the workplace only 'eight' hours, they strived to be very productive during that time, so they didn't waste a single minute.

After two days of intense and exhausting work, Gerard and Robert appeared triumphant: they had finished writing down all the tasks.

"Companions!" roared Robert. "I introduce the work to be done. The tasks to be done are these, and in this order. They are prioritized by the value they provide to the client, and their order is not negotiable. But, as you are the ones that are going to do them, it will be you who will estimate them. You have the power to do it. Who are empowered?"

"We are!" answered they all in chorus.

"We are going to prepare the work that we commit to carry out in the first iteration. We will estimate task after task, and, when we believe we have enough work for two weeks, we'll stop and that will be the content of the first iteration, that is to say, the first 'Sprint Backlog'. Any questions?" No one answered, so Robert finished the conversation. "Well, so let's estimate! Gerard will play the role of 'Product Owner', because he is the one who knows the most and who is most in touch with the client. If you have any doubts, he is your man."

They all quickly locked themselves in the large meeting room and began to estimate the tasks. They set up a very enriching dialogue, where everyone gave their opinion, some because the task was estimated in less time, others because they saw it as more complex and wanted to give it in more time. In the end, everyone ended up aligning and reaching an agreement.

They were like this all the afternoon. Robert and Gerard were present all the time but didn't intervene, making it clear that the team was empowered to estimate the tasks. Gerard was asked from time to time to clarify doubts so they could discover the real scope of the tasks.

Finally, when they saw that they had enough work for the next two weeks, with a steady and sustainable pace (without doing overtime), they ended the meeting and went home very happy. They knew what they were going to do for the next two weeks. As they had estimated among all the teammates, they committed to carry out the number of tasks they knew they could surely carry out, and all this without suffering the dreaded overtime.

"Well, Gerard, this has just begun."

"I'm scared to death, Rob. I hope you know what you are doing. It makes a lot of sense, but I'm afraid to be risking my job."

Antonio Montes Orozco

"It is an act of faith, Gerard. Remove fear from the equation. It's going to be fine. The teammates have estimated the tasks, and we haven't intervened, so they have really committed, because they were involved in the decision. That is very powerful and cannot fail. You now have a team of eight members fully committed to the project. Remember to let them participate in every decision you make, and they will commit to that decision."

The following weeks, everything went on as planned. The way of chopping up the tasks left Gerard very calm, because, even if the experiment went wrong, at least he knew that the team would be working on what would bring the most value to the client, so they would see tangible results and wouldn't get angry.

The first iteration ended, and they showed the client what they had. This surprised the client a lot, because they weren't used to seeing things working with only part of the system requirements. The client was eager to see the next delivery of software running and began to clarify what type of final product they wanted, so they gave the team a very valuable feedback that led the project towards an optimal result.

Robert didn't work overtime again, so he came home every day in a good mood, wishing to talk to Victoria.

"Hi, Vicky."

"Hi, dear," replied Vicky, who gave Robert a loud welcome kiss. "You won't believe it, but today I had an interview and I think they will hire me."

"Vicky, that's amazing! Well, if you want, we evangelize them in 'Agilism'."

"You're too silly!" said Victoria, laughing.

"Well, now that you've found a job, we can create a real family. How about having a child?"

"Are you serious?"

"Well, of course. Eliminate fear from the equation and let's go ahead."

"Rob, you've finally decided!" Victoria hugged Robert, crying with joy.

Antonio Montes Orozco

Epilogue

Three years later we find Robert and Victoria, in the afternoon, in a park next to their house, enjoying a beautiful girl.

"Sophia, watch out for the swing, it's very tall," says Robert in a soft voice.

"Baby hears a fart," replies Sophia, the beautiful daughter of Robert and Victoria.

"Well, in the end, so much cauliflower and so much broccoli had its consequences. I created an eschatological girl," says Robert. "Do you feel like pooping, my love?"

"No, Rob, look at the dog there, it's barking. She meant 'bark', instead of 'fart', "Victoria makes him see."

"Ha, ha, ha, ha," laughs Robert. "Thanks god. I believed that so much cauliflower had effected her."

"Ha, ha, ha, ha, how silly you are!"

In the end Robert did not have to leave the company, but it ended up adopting "Scrum", the framework that Stephen had taught him. The projects always went well now, and Robert came home every day early enough to play with Sophia and spend a pleasant afternoon with his family. He did not fall ill again, because the daily intake of fruit gave him all the vitamins he needed. He had lost the extra pounds and exercised at home frequently, so he felt very well, apart from balanced and happy with his life.

Antonio Montes Orozco

Sophia's arrival had put the young couple to the test, who now knew what it was to get little sleep and not respite at home, but Sophia's love more than made up for this effort.

Victoria was still working, so they had to be helped by a daycare and grandparents but, as the saying goes: 'If you love the work, it's not work'. Sophia was everyone's joy.

And, eliminating fear from the equation...

"Come on, Bowling Ball, let's go home," said Robert to Victoria.

"But, Rob, do you think it's polite to call me that, your dear five-month-pregnant wife? Oh, I see, you aren't serious."

"Look what happens when you eliminate fear from the equation; from a cute little daughter, we will move on to two little ones. What awaits poor Charles: a sister who rages him and parents who will eat him with kisses. This is priceless, really. It is clear that Agilism and broccoli combine very well."

"Ha, ha, ha, ha, ha, ha!" laughed Victoria and Robert.

Antonio Montes Orozco

Conclusion

On this journey through the life of Robert and Victoria, we have learned the following:

- The five steps that cascade into what I call "The Work Stress Cycle".

- The principle of "eliminate fear from the equation".

- The great secret of the human being: we can reinvent ourselves and be as we want.

"The Work Stress Cycle"

It all starts with unforeseen or even bad management, which lead to having to extend the working day. This is the **first step: the lengthening of the workday**.

Apart from our professional life, we have a range of obligations in our personal lives, which must be taken care of. Being late prevents us from attending to these obligations, so our private life begins to limp, and this causes us to lose our balance. This is the **second step: imbalance with our personal life**.

We begin to notice the stress, because we work hard and our personal life limps. Our body reveals itself and demands down time, something that evades us. But we do not have free time, so we escape at the cost of our sleep. This is the **third step: lack of sleep**. This lack of sleep leads us to three physiological consequences:

- Negativity, because we remember only the bad, and stop storing pleasant experiences.

- Obesity, because the endocrine system is deregulated, so we tend to gain weight. Such overweight, prolonged over time (years), can lead to a stroke or a heart attack.

- Disease. Lack of sleep lowers our defenses, and it's easy for us to get a cold or a flu.

The weakened health and extreme tiredness cause our performance at work to suffer, so we began to make many mistakes. This is the **fourth step: the deterioration of work performance**.

Entering the fourth step, the professional career suffers, because we do not perform fully, our personal life is already resentful, and our health is deteriorated, so we have fallen into a destructive spiral, which is the **fifth step**: the **burning out** or **"work stress cycle"**.

We have reached the fifth step starting with a pace of work that was not sustainable. Therefore, we must look for work rhythms that are constant and sustainable, as recommended by "Agilism". In this way we will avoid entering the first step.

Therefore, the recipe to avoid the work stress cycle is **to keep a steady and sustainable pace, and work very efficiently**.

Antonio Montes Orozco

Eliminate Fear From The Equation

Fear immobilizes us and prevents us from thinking clearly. Making decisions while allowing ourselves to be influenced by fear, means we could be wrong, and be at the mercy of external manipulations.

Throughout life we are afraid of dying, so we abandon proven medical treatments that are born of the scientific method, and instead fall into the fallacy of pseudosciences that are useless, and that can accelerate our passage to the next life.

We are also afraid of losing our livelihood, so we fall into the networks of manipulators at work, which lead us to lack of coordination and chaos, forcing us into overtime.

Therefore "eliminate fear from the equation" when making decisions: you'll see that you will make more accurate decisions.

The human beings can reinvent themselves and decide how they want to be

The idea that "you are what you are, and cannot be changed" is spread throughout society. It is a big mistake, because the brain of the human being is tremendously malleable, so we can always acquire new habits.

Actually, what holds the false belief that "you are what you are" is the justification for not fighting. Notice that we are throwing in the towel from the beginning, quieting our conscience and justifying ourselves not acting. Well, learn that you can achieve what you set out to do, so be careful with what you want, as you will achieve it.

Antonio Montes Orozco

Special Thanks

As I did in my first book (*Scrum for Non-Techies*), I will thank all those who have supported me so much in alphabetical order. First of all, I thank my mother for teaching me the service and concern for those around me, making me a natural Scrum Master (facilitator leader of 'Agilism'). Secondly, I thank my father, who is watching us from heaven, for his teaching on how to keep a steady and sustainable pace that allows us to achieve our dreams without getting exhausted. The truth is that both taught me, as a child, that the most important thing was to fight for the family.

Thirdly, I thank Jessie Sanders for his masterful review of the text, and his unconditional support. Besides, without Jessie, this English version would never have seen the light.

And last but not least, I thank Rosa for the patience she's had with me, because writing a book implies many hours in which one cannot be available for the family.

To all of them, my infinite thanks. And for you, dear reader, who has had the patience to read this work, my eternal thanks.

Antonio Montes Orozco

About the Author

Antonio Montes Orozco was born in Madrid, Spain, in 1972. He studied Telecommunications Engineering at the Polytechnic University of Madrid.

He began his first steps in the world of work as a systems administrator, specializing in the Solaris, HPUX and AIX operating systems. After a few years as a systems administrator, he started programming in C++ and, in 2006, he learned about the Scrum methodology and was one of the pioneers in its application in Spain. Since then he has been working as a Scrum Master and as a coach to implement this methodology.

He ended up working in a major Spanish financial institution, where he introduced Scrum in one of the Business areas.

He was certified in 2015 by the prestigious PMI (Project Management Institute), as a practitioner of Agile (ACP: Agile Certified Practitioner), and by Scrum Manager in 2014.

In 2016 he obtained the Executive Master in Management of Information Technologies, by the Institute of Business Executives (IDE-CESEM) of Spain.

Credits

The Work Stress Cycle: a business fable about "coaching", "agilism" and the five steps that lead to burn out at work.

Antonio Montes Orozco

First edition in e-book: March 2020

ISBN: 979-8-62-952693-3

www.ingramcontent.com/pod-product-compliance
Lightning Source LLC
Chambersburg PA
CBHW021454210526
45463CB00002B/773